Have you danced the round dance yet?

It's always been my favorite one.

My Moosum and my Kokum

Let me dance it to the rising sun.

We set our tipi by the creek

Where Moosum wakes me every day,

When first the sun caresses the earth

And draws us all outside to pray.

Ki-piciyin ci ceskwa

Kakike oma e-cikiyitaman

Nimosom ekwa Nohkom

E-pakitincik ta-nimihitoyan isko pe-wapahki

Nimanokanan ciki sipisis

Nimosom e-koskonit tahto kisikaw

Mayo pisim pe-nokosici

Kakiyaw wayawitimihk kikakisimonaw

# The Drum Calls Softly

BY

**DAVID BOUCHARD**

AND

**SHELLEY WILLIER**

PAINTINGS BY

**JIM POITRAS**

SINGING AND DRUMMING BY

**NORTHERN CREE**

*Red Deer* PRESS

Step into the outer circle

Listen to the beating drum.

Take my hand and hold it tight

The thing you seek is soon to come.

Everybody's smiling because

Our hearts all beat as one.

Listen to the drum – it calls

The magic's here – it has begun . . .


Pitikwe-takiske ota kawasikamepowiyak

Nitotow e-matwehit mistikwaskihk

Otina nicihciy ekwa sihtaskinskenin

Anima kanitonaman kekac takosin

Piko-awiyak chikiyitam osam

Kakiyaw miteha peyakwan ematwechik

Nitotow mistikwaskihk, e-tepwasiwet

Emamahtaw totamihk ota, macihtaniwi

We start the day by giving thanks
To mother earth for all she brings.
Then Kokum takes to working
By the fire – I can hear her sing.
She's making Bannock; we all stop
To eat together by the creek;
When soon she bids us gather round:
*"I hear the water start to speak."*

Ka-mahcitaya kisikaw e-nanaskomoweya
Ohci nikawiynan aski ka-mikowiyak piko-kikway
Aham ekwa Nohkom e-maci atosket
Ciki iskotew – nipetawaw e-nikamot
E-hosihat pakwesikan; Ninakinan
E-mamow micisoyak ciki sipisi
E-tepwatikoyak ka-mamopayiyak
*"Ma, nipeten nipiy e-maci pikiskwet."*

*"That creek – it speaks in circles*
*You must shut your eyes and try to hear.*
*It's telling of how seasons turn*
*And how they have from year to year.*
*And now, it speaks of a baby's birth*
*And now, an elder's place to rest*
*And now, it speaks of olden days*
*And now, of raven's sacred quest."*

*"Anima sipisis – ewasikam pikiskwet*
*Piko kakipahaman kiskisikwa ekwa*
   *ka-kwenitotaman*
*E-wihta aski meskwacipayowina*
*Kakike*
*Eko ekwa e-atota awasis e-nahtawikit*
*Eko ekwa kitehyayah e-ayiwepit*
*Eko ekwa emamskota kayas*
*Eko ekwa kahkakiw nitawi natononikewin."*

I find I'm getting thirsty

When the creek invites me down to drink.

My body soothed – I feel content

My soul is cleansed – I'm free to think.

I bid my Kokum to come near

And ask if she can hear at all

I whisper softly, *"Can you hear*

*The circles in my heart – they call???"*

Nimositan e-nohteyapakweyan

Ahaw sipisis nitomik tanto minikweyan

Nimiyo-macihon nimiyaw ekakecihak

Nitahcahk ekanatak, nimiyo-macihon

Nintomaw Nohkom ciki ka-peyitotet

Nikwecimaw kispin epetak

Nikimoci-pikiskwan, *"Kipeten niteh etitipewehak –*

    *etepwaticik???"*

Dance in circles around the drum
Seek the magic and it will come.
Shut your eyes so you might hear
That song is sung to draw you near.

Dance real hard around that drum
Feel the magic . . . it's here; it has come
It's right here, deep inside of you
I know you feel it – because I do too.

Nimihitok wasakam mistikwaskihk
Ka-peyitotew kispin kinintonen mamatawisin.
Kipaha kiskisikwa ka-kipeten
Animanima nikamowin ka-petotayikon cikik

Sohkesimow waskam mistikwaskihk
Mamatawisin anima kamositan . . .
    takosiw; ota astew
Ekota anima astew kimiyaw
Nikiskiyiten emositayan – osam nista nimositan.

The early evening brings out friends

Who come with hugs and warm handshakes;

With caring smiles and laughter too

And stories and songs; some old and some new.

How high can eagle fly? – they sing.

How long can bear lay there asleep?

The drum knows all – we hear it speak.

It answers us with every beat.


Mihcit kiwicewakanak ka-nokosowak otakosiki

Kape akwaskitinkewak ekwa ka-atamiskakewak;

Kape papiw-nakosiwak ekwa kapahpowak

Ekwa acimowina ekwa nikamowina;

    atiht kayasa ekwa atiht oskaya.


Enikamocik tanimayikohk ki-pimihaw kihew?

Tanimayikohk maskwa ka-kinipaw?

Mistikwaskihk kiskeyitam piko kikway –

    nipapetenan epapikiskwet.

Enaskohtowet ka-matwehit.

Night has finally taken hold
I'm tired but I feel warm and good.
My Moosum and my Kokum
Lead me home the way I knew they would.

I'm weary I can hardly walk;
When I hear a voice that calls my name.
I stumble as I turn to look
*"Come back my friend. You're not the same."*

E-ati-tipiskak
Ninestosin maka nimiyo-macihon.
Nimosom ekwa Nohkom
Nikiwetayikwak nikiskiyiten ekosi ketotamok.

Ninestosin etatow epimohteyan;
Ketatawe kapetaman niwihowin awiyak etepwasit.
Nipiswahcahikan e-ati-kweskiyan ewi-kitapataman
*"Astam niwicewakan, namoya kiya peyakwan."*

Whose voice is this? – I ask myself.
Is it the creek or is it still the drum?
I listen hard and I try to think
It's from my heart it seems to come.

Awina awa otehtakosiwin, ekwecimisoyan?
Sipisis ci apo acipiko mistikwaskihk?
Nisohki nitoten ekwa nikwe-mamitoniyiten
Nitehik ohci e-otakotek.

Have you danced the round dance yet?
Of course you have – you're in my dream.
You've danced in circles next to me
You now know things aren't as they seem.

Ki-piciyin ci ceskwa?
Tapwe kitoten asay – ki-pawatin.
Ki-wici-wawasikamsimomin
Kimamoweyiten ekwa namoya piko kikway
    peyakwan eteyihtakwak.

Your heart and mine have beat as one
We've danced all night around that drum.
You held my hand and you stayed with me.
You now are family; you're a part of me.

Kiteh ekwa niteh peyakwan e-matwecik
Kiwapan wasikasimowinaw mistikwaskihk.
E-sakinskeniyin ekwa ekisaci wiciwiyin.
Peyakwan niwakomakan ekwa kiya.

*For Chris Patrick – my agent and friend – who allows me to live my dreams!*   DAVID BOUCHARD

*To my father Peter, who enriches my life with his love, support, and storytelling.*   SHELLEY WILLIER

*With love, I dedicate this to my three granddaughters and great-granddaughter.*   JIM POITRAS

*To my late father who gave me the means and the gift to see many places and meet*
*many people who would become honored friends. The gift of language and song.*   STEVE WOOD

Text copyright © 2008 David Bouchard & Shelley Willier
Illustration copyright © 2008 Jim Poitras
Music copyright © 2008 Northern Cree

5 4 3 2 1

PUBLISHED BY
Red Deer Press
A Fitzhenry & Whiteside Company
1512, 1800–4 Street S.W.
Calgary, Alberta, Canada T2S 2S5
www.reddeerpress.com

Cree translation by Steve Wood, Northern Cree
Book design by Arifin Graham, Alaris Design
Sound design and mastering by Geoff Edwards – streamworks.ca
Flute by David Bouchard
Photographs by Anatol Dreyer
Printed and bound in Hong Kong, China

ACKNOWLEDGMENTS
Financial support provided by the Canada Council, and the Government of Canada
through the Book Publishing Industry Development Program (BPIDP).

THE CANADA COUNCIL | LE CONSEIL DES ARTS
FOR THE ARTS | DU CANADA
SINCE 1957 | DEPUIS 1957

LIBRARY AND ARCHIVES CANADA CATALOGUING IN PUBLICATION
Bouchard, David, 1952–
The drum calls softly / David Bouchard & Shelley Willier ;
paintings by Jim Poitras ; music by Northern Cree.
Accompanied by a CD featuring the music of Northern Cree.
ISBN 978-0-88995-421-2
　　1. Cree dance—Juvenile fiction. 2. Cree Indians—Juvenile fiction.
I. Willier, Shelley II. Poitras, Jim III. Northern Cree Singers IV. Title.
PS8553.O759D78 2008　　　　　jC813'.54　　　　C2008-900366-7

UNITED STATES CATALOGUING-IN-PUBLICATION DATA
Bouchard, David.
　　The drum calls softly / David Bouchard ; Shelley Willier ;
paintings by Jim Poitras ; music by Northern Cree.
[32] p. : col. illus. ; cm.
Includes compact disc of story.
ISBN 978-088995-421-2
I. Willier, Shelley. II. Poitras, Jim. III. Title.
[E] dc22　PZ7.B6734　2008